# maximizing wealth for chiropractors

TODD CALAMITA, *CFP*®

For permissions, contact: Todd Calamita, todd@calamitawealth.com

Visit the author's website: calamitawealth.com



Book Format, Illustrations, & Cover Design: Melody Christian, Finicky Designs
Book Editor: Sharyn Ellison

ISBN: 978-0-578-43443-8

# TABLE OF CONTENTS

# INTRODUCTION

When I was 16 years old my dad took me to meet a financial advisor for the first time – and I discovered that **investing was magic**. I had saved up what I considered a "bunch" of money from my landscaping business. I recall sitting across from the advisor when he told me that for every $666 I invested I would get $1000 back in four years. (Keep in mind this was the 80's and interest rates were around 12%.) I couldn't believe what I was hearing. I said, "You mean I don't have to cut lawns or do any work? They just give me back another $334?"

"Yes, that's how it works."

"I'll take four of those!" I said. And that was my first official foray into investing. I ultimately kept that money locked away until I graduated college. But I'll never forget that moment of realization that my money could make money – with virtually no effort on my part!

This passion for smart money strategies – and for helping people – has informed my career as a financial advisor. Growing up lower middle class in a family with little money for extras, I learned early on to be frugal and motivated. I started my first business at age 10, paid my own way through college, and worked in the investment side of money management until I decided that getting my Certified Financial Planner (CFP) license would provide knowledge that really has the power to help people. **I wanted to help people accomplish their goals and dreams in life.**

My experience with chiropractors has only increased my respect for the profession. I admire this healing profession and see its value both personally and society-wide. Especially given today's opioid crisis, chiropractors are even more necessary as an alternative to drugs and unnecessary surgery. **Chiropractors can help solve our overmedicated society, bring health care costs down, and give people better quality of life.**

My wife, Teresa, saw a wonderful chiropractor throughout her pregnancy. One day, around 12 weeks into the pregnancy, Teresa could barely breathe or get out of bed due to extreme mid-back pain. Her chiropractor, who specializes in maternity care, got us in right away. She looked at Teresa for about 20 seconds and said, "I know what the issue is. It's going to be painful to fix it, is that ok? A rib is out of place." She did an adjustment, popped it back in, and Teresa felt immediate relief. This experience was a world away from going to the ER, where we would have likely been subjected to X-rays and more invasive procedures.

**My respect for chiropractors and experience in helping small businesses thrive has led me to seek out ways to help chiropractors engage in smart financial planning strategies.**

Let's face it, most chiropractic practices are small businesses run by people who aren't necessarily passionate about the minutia of running a small business. Understandably, their focus is on a very specialized skill set that more than likely does not include running cash flow analyses or managing employees. This too often leads to struggling practices dealing with cash flow crises that could lead to insufficient funds on which to retire. I am committed to helping those in the healing arts understand how to best handle the financial side of their practices so they can devote more energy to what they do best – **helping people.**

*- Todd Calamita*

# PART I:

# PLANNING TO WIN

# CHAPTER 1:

# FINANCIAL PLANNING AND YOUR VALUES

*"If money go before, all ways do lie open."*

**–William Shakespeare**

Chiropractic in the U.S. is a $15 billion industry that has grown at a rate of 1.1% over the past five years. While the overall industry shows slow but steady growth, the reality on the ground for many chiropractors is a frantic scramble to keep their heads above water coupled by an overwhelming desire to help their patients heal and support their families. But these efforts, while noble, often come at the cost of smart, proactive financial planning. In the daily, sometimes overwhelming, details of running a business and attending to patients and staff, it's easy to become distracted from the preparation required to achieve long-terms goals.

The fact is, the money you earn today – this month, this year – can have a transformative effect on your future and the people you cherish. But today's busy chiropractors often lack the time or expertise necessary to take a comprehensive, or holistic, approach when it comes to financial planning. Protecting and building your wealth requires a team of professionals who can create a coordinated strategy to ensure a lifetime of financial success.

Most of us have experienced financial planning on an ad hoc basis: when to buy or sell a certain investment or setting up an IRA, for example. But when considering holistic financial planning or wealth management, a deeper journey is required. The challenges of today's healthcare professionals are complex and may involve debt avoidance, equity creation, tax mitigation, income insurance, investment strategies, and more. For this reason, it's important to seek out a financial advisor who will help achieve your goals by coordinating all of the various aspects of your financial life. Remember, this is not simply about asset management. More important, it's about your *values*.

## chapter 1

# HOLISTIC FINANCIAL PLANNING

You would never treat one part of the body without considering the whole. Similarly, the best financial advisors are committed to gaining a holistic sense of each client's needs. Besides inquiring into your income, savings, debt burden, and current investments, they should ask questions such as:

- What's important to you about money?
- What are your personal goals?
- What are your professional goals?
- What do you do (or want to do) for your children?
- Ideally, where would you like to be when you are 45? 55? 65? 75?
- What are your quality-of-life desires (houses, travel, boats, cars)?
- How often do you want an overall review of your financial situation and progress toward your goals?
- What charitable causes do you donate to? Volunteer for?
- What do you want to do for the world at large?

This broad inquiry is a crucial step in creating customized financial services and solutions that address your needs as a successful chiropractor. Because, like the body, the various aspects of your financial life are interdependent and require thoughtful care and maintenance.

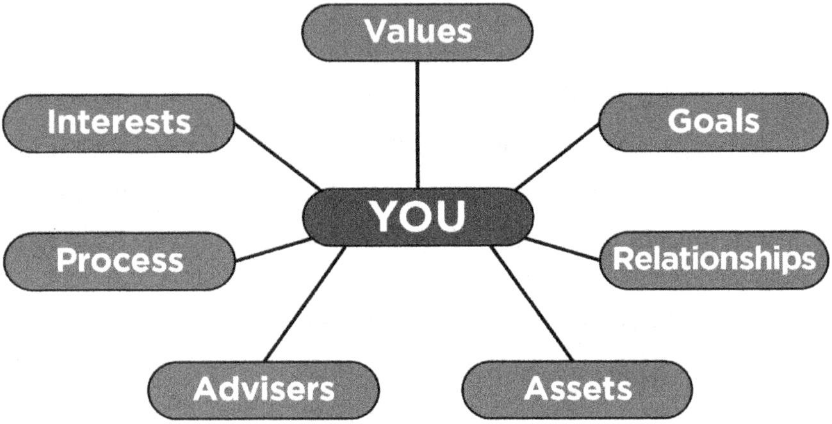


Still, it can be tempting to put off holistic financial planning for another day, especially when immediate concerns such as patient retention, marketing strategies, and monthly cash flow issues are top of mind. Where do you start? When considering the "big picture" of smart wealth management, it can be helpful to break it down into the following simple formula: Wealth Management = Investment Consulting + Advanced Planning + Relationship Management. **WM = IC + AP + RM**

- **Investment Consulting** – Sound investment strategies can help grow and preserve your wealth. A continual assessment of where your assets can best perform, taking into account time horizons and risk tolerance, is the foundation of savvy financial planning.

- **Advanced Planning** – Beyond investing, there are other financial challenges that are of importance to today's successful chiropractors. These include: Wealth Enhancement (managing cash flow and tax mitigation), Wealth Transfer (passing down wealth), Wealth Protection (risk mitigation and insurance), and Charitable Giving (supporting causes that are personally meaningful).
- **Relationship Management** – Your needs are varied and will change over time. These interrelated challenges will require the ongoing coordination and collaboration between a team of trusted legal, tax, insurance, and investment advisors.

Though vital, too few chiropractors approach their financial lives from this holistic perspective. Instead they – often unwittingly – allow things to fall through the cracks. This unfortunate reality can lead to a myriad of problems, such as paying too much in taxes, not being able to retire on time, loss of financial freedom, ongoing stress about money, and not being able to pass on wealth as desired.

The other option: positioning your money to achieve that which you value the most – peace of mind and financial freedom for you and your family.

# ACHIEVING FINANCIAL PEACE

Money is not just a number, nor is it simply a symbol of your hard work. Rather, money is a tool to achieve your dreams for yourself and your family, whether tangible (a vacation house) or intangible (freedom from anxiety). Many chiropractors wish they had a greater sense of control over their finances, a sense of peace and progress. In this book, we will cover many topics having to do with financial planning, but to start, ask yourself: *What concerns me the most today financially?*

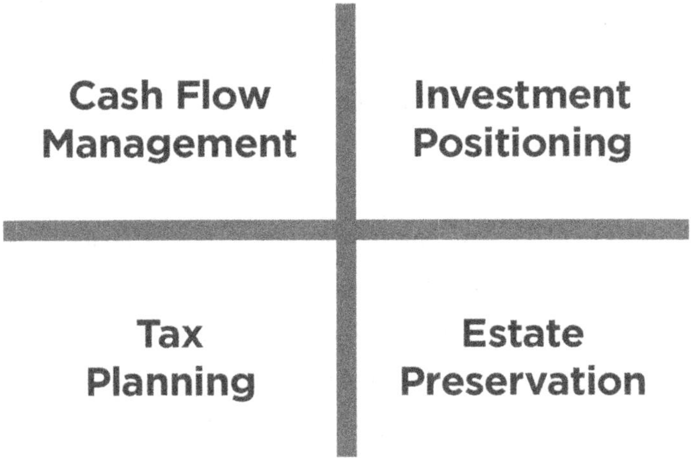


**Cash Flow Management.** Perhaps your biggest concern is how to manage your day-to-day business in a realistic, balanced way. Chiropractors tend to struggle with cash flow problems, in part, because they often don't appreciate the difference between collections and cash flow. This may lead them to overspend in areas like salaries, rent, equipment purchases, and marketing. To make matters worse, many DCs underestimate the amount of money they need to set aside for taxes throughout the year. Not knowing exactly how much money is coming in every month, coupled with the outlay of overhead and staff salaries, can lead to a sense of constant strain and worry. In fact, 82% of businesses that go under fail because of cash flow problems.[1] Achieving a streamlined and efficient cash flow system with the right staff, software, or your own self-discipline can lift a cloud of daily anxiety.

**Investment Positioning.** The question of how to grow your money is a concern many chiropractors have. Should you be aggressive in your approach to investing or play it safe? Your investment strategies will depend on your attitude toward risk, but should ultimately seek to stay in harmony with major market trends with a focus on guarding against large long term loss. How you allocate your investments should also be informed by your age, as well as your retirement goals.

**Tax Planning.** Because many of the near 170,000 chiropractors in the U.S. are small business owners or self-employed, taxes can feel especially burdensome and complex. Due to the ever-changing tax code, you must focus on yearly tax planning as part of your total financial package. With knowledge and discipline, as well as a good CPA, tax planning can become less of a worry.

**Estate Preservation.** Chiropractors care deeply about their families and want to ensure their legacies are solidly in place. Proper estate planning is the capstone in developing your long-range strategy, and helps you control and protect your legacy. Without planning for your estate, you cannot guarantee your wish for how your assets are allocated. But thoughtful preparation, on the other hand, can have long-term benefits for your loved ones and your community.

When you become informed and disciplined regarding the above four categories, you will gain a better sense of financial control, thus conquering feelings of overwhelm and worry about the future. What an unburdening that will be!

Whatever your financial focus may be, taking time to assess *who you are* should be the first step to creating a plan that leads you to your financial objectives. After all, your personal concerns and goals will inform what you want to prioritize.

Whether you're just out of school, in the middle of building your practice, or are on the verge of retirement – smart financial planning is a responsibility as well as a privilege. You owe it to yourself and your loved ones to find the right person to guide you through the often confusing and intimidating waters of wealth management, because like the well-being of your patients, the power to achieve your goals is in your hands.

# CHAPTER 2:

# THE POWER AND PAIN OF DEBT

*"A man in debt is so far a slave."*

**- Ralph Waldo Emerson**

Here are some scary facts: As of March 2014, American consumers owed $11.52 trillion in debt. The two largest sources of this massive number are mortgage and student loan debt, with credit card debt coming in third with $856.5 billion owed. If these numbers are hard to fathom, consider this breakdown: the average U.S. household owes $7,115 on their credit cards.[2]

Debt is especially insidious for chiropractors, many of whom begin their careers carrying an enormous amount of student loan debt. Consider this: in the past, chiropractic college used to cost a mere $325 for each term, whereas today's chiropractors customarily carry student loans of over $200,000.[3] Adding to the debt impact on the profession, today's world is high-tech, and the chiropractic industry is no exception. From complex tables to laser therapy devices to muscle stimulation machines – the equipment patients now expect typically requires financing.

The desire to grow your practice can add to your debt burden if not approached with care. Does that X-ray machine or new therapy device bring in enough income to offset the interest you are still paying on it? Do you owe any back taxes? In your personal realm, what "toys" do you enjoy? A car or boat payment is definitely a debt. A mortgage is a debt – yes, even if you pay it in full every month.

We all know, reflexively, that debt is "bad," especially when it comes to credit card debt, with its jumbo interest rates and the way the industry (if not our society at large) encourages paying the minimum now as a way to "get ahead." I'll go through the troubling side of debt first. Then I'll also explore the good side of having liabilities. Debt, when used in a savvy way, can be helpful. It's all about having the financial knowhow and commitment to manage that debt and stay on top of it.

chapter 2

# AVOIDING DEBT

The burden of debt can affect more than just your financial life. It carries a significant emotional and physical toll and can erode your confidence. Life milestones such as launching your own practice, buying a first home – or that longed-for vacation home – are often put off or don't come to pass at all when you have a substantial debt load. Down the road, your liabilities can really hurt: according to Dr. Tom Necela, author of *The Ultimate Chiropractic Exit Strategy*, only 5% of all chiropractors can afford to maintain their current lifestyle when they retire.[4] And this is in spite of those in the profession making above average incomes! Given these repercussions, the wisdom of avoiding debt entirely seems obvious.

Of course, sometimes debt can be a necessary burden (think school loans, mortgages, and office leases), but there are ways to avoid making the easy mistakes that so often trip up those in the chiropractic community. Here are five realistic habits that I suggest every chiropractor adopt in order to avoid becoming mired in debt.

- Track what you spend.
- Decide ahead of time how much you want to spend on a certain item *before* inviting a vendor representative to your practice.

- Determine for the year how much you want to spend on large-ticket items such as vacations and home improvement.
- Don't put anything on credit.
- Do not make spontaneous large purchases. Sleep on it first and then decide if you really want to spend the money – even if you have the money to spend!

## LIVING WITHIN YOUR MEANS

Ready for a little tough love? Chiropractors tend to be a social community, many of whom frequent conferences and enjoy hearing about each other's lives and practices. But here's what often happens: say you're chatting with a fellow doctor at a recent professional gathering. He regales you with stories of his recent trip to Italy, then his kitchen renovation. When he drives off in his BMW 6 Series convertible, you're left with the impression that this guy has "made it," that he is a rich chiropractor.

But here's the reality – no one at these events is talking about their take-home pay. Without seeing his books, this apparently wealthy doctor may actually be swimming in debt and interest payments that will eventually take down his practice. The façade is simply that: a façade.

Whether this tendency to live above one's means is due to an inferiority complex among chiropractors, a lack of financial know-how, or some combination of the two, the profession does have more than its fair share of hidden debt burden among the seemingly "high flyers." One contributing factor may be the culture of gimmicky proposition that is rife within the industry. With sales people consistently trying to sell chiropractors questionable products – from life insurance to financial products to body creams – it can start to feel normal to choose the latest, newfangled solution over the staider options of maxing out a 401K, having a consistent plan for paying off current debts, and drinking plenty of water.

Resisting the trap of ostentation takes a combination of will power, planning, and some straight talk. Ask yourself: *Can I really afford this?* Will a $50,000 car send you further into debt – and further away from a happy retirement – when a $20,000 vehicle would do? Then ask: *Who am I really trying to impress?* The only one you should be worried about impressing is your future self. Imagine the financial peace and security you will gain by living a debt free life!

## WHEN YOU'RE IN TOO DEEP

Unfortunately, finding yourself in the quicksand of debt is an all too common experience for chiropractors these days. A combination of student loans, aggressive credit card companies, and the above-discussed temptation to live above one's means puts too many practices at real risk. That said, it's never too late to fight your way out of debt – no matter how bottomless it feels.

Should you find yourself in this situation, the key is to take baby steps. First, go ahead and tear up those credit cards. No more purchasing items unless you have the *actual* cash to do so. Then prioritize which debts you'd like to pay off – begin by tackling the card with the highest interest rate and work your way down from there. Take the savings earned from each loan paid off to then excise another. Along the way, you may want to go ahead and knock out one of your smaller loans in order to give yourself a lift and build momentum. Here's another secret to paying off debt: make small payments whenever you can. Banks want you to pay on a monthly basis so they can collect the total interest for the month. Making more frequent payments beats them at their game.[5]

You may be thinking this all seems impossible, given mammoth interest rates. If so, it's time to look at your cash flow and figure out how you can either cut your spending or bring in extra money. Can you trade in your car for one that requires a lower payment? Do some research – is it possible to get a deferment or forbearance on your student loan, at least for the time being? And avoid unnecessary expenses such as eating out and vacations.

While none of these solutions is fun, the point is that it is crucial to do everything possible to reduce your bad debt and the harmful financial, emotional, and physical repercussions it can have on your life. Put a debt reduction plan in place that you don't have to think about – and then stick with it. It may take 15-20 years to pay off your liabilities, but don't let that overwhelm you. Whether you're 30, 45, or 62, heading towards a debt-free life can mean massive benefits for your long-term wealth. Think about it this way: every dollar that goes toward your interest payments could instead be bolstering your retirement account. And wouldn't you rather invest in your family's future than simply handing your money over to MasterCard?

There is one path to becoming debt-free that I do not recommend – declaring bankruptcy. In most circumstances, becoming this deeply mired in debt is the result of a series of poor choices, poor planning, and bad luck. If you feel yourself headed down this path, do your best to turn the ship around before it's too late. Bankruptcy is a last resort option that leaves a black mark on your credit for 10 years and can also negatively affect your self-esteem. No matter how deep your debt, there is value in owning up to what you owe rather than taking the easy way out. A better option for the most severe cases of bad debt is negotiating with creditors for better terms or consulting a credit counselor. This can be a smart way to get the ball rolling.

# THE GOOD SIDE OF DEBT

I believe in debt for the right reasons – or, making your money work for you, rather than you working for your money. This can mean making sound choices – even if there is risk involved – about investing in your education, a home, or launching your own practice. Or, it can mean putting your money to profitable use rather than paying off a low-interest bearing debt.

Getting a loan to start or expand your own practice can be a good strategy for building your chiropractic career. Just be sure to keep in mind the alternatives for paying back the debt if the practice fails. Indeed, this debt could become your personal burden. If you keep this fact in the back of your mind, you may make more prudent choices when it comes to the amount of money you borrow in the first place. A thorough business plan and understanding of your market will be key to minimizing risk in this situation. Remember: it's easy to get carried away and buy equipment you don't necessarily need to get your practice up and running. Spend as little as you can and build your practice step by step. That said, borrowing to fund a specific need can also be a smart way to make more money in the end. If your market is missing a chiropractic practice that features cold laser therapy, for example, the initial investment into this service can eventually be paid off and will help increase overall profits.

Borrowing money can bolster your ability to excel at your career, build your home equity, and grow your investment portfolio. With a little bit of luck and plenty of hard work, hopefully the good debts you acquire (and pay off) will help you to achieve the ultimate goal: financial peace with a liability-free retirement.

## BUYING VS. LEASING

Investing in a space for your practice will likely necessitate a hefty bank loan. Smart research about what and where you are buying, depending on current interest rates, can make borrowing this money a no-brainer – you're building equity while avoiding paying a monthly lease.

That said, when you are considering whether to buy property for your practice or leasing a space, take special consideration of all the ramifications. This choice is a crucial one for chiropractors and must be approached from a cash flow perspective. Look at the numbers: if it costs $1,500 per month to rent a space and a mortgage payment for similar space will set you back $2,500 per month, that's a significant hit to your monthly take-home. Sure, you're building equity, but you will also shoulder the property taxes and other inevitable headaches that come along with owning real estate. Run the numbers and make sure they work. After all, a mortgage is a significant liability, especially if you also carry one for your home.

Chiropractors are drawn to the idea of purchasing office space for a number of reasons, two of which are questionable. First, there is often a sense of peer pressure in the industry. "If that guy across town bought, I should too!" In reality, what the other guy is doing has no relevance to your business because – again – you can't see the bald reality of his bottom line. Second, many doctors assume that the money made from the eventual sale of the space will in the end fund their retirement. This is simply a pipe dream, for a variety of reasons, but primarily because for every one chiropractor that wants into the business there are 10 looking to leave.[6] Talk about a buyer's market!

According to Dr. Necela, chiropractors often have less than optimal exit strategies for leaving the profession. Critically, most decide to sell when their business is waning or their health is failing, rather than when the practice is at its peak performance. A thriving business, among other economic factors, drives up the sales price. But poor planning – or a lack of planning altogether – means that instead of selling your office space for a ton of money at just the right moment, other, less optimal outcomes occur: the associate to whom you hoped to pass on the business abandons ship, you have to keep working longer than you want, you have to sell your practice for peanuts. (There are many factors at work in successfully exiting your practice. For more information, I highly recommend Dr. Necela's book, *The Ultimate Chiropractic Exit Strategy*.)

***

Achieving the optimal balance of good and bad debt is an ongoing, delicate dance. As we know, real estate bubbles can burst and businesses fail. Your market could dry up or you could face a medical crisis. Life is full of uncertainties. The only way to mitigate these risks is to live thoughtfully, ask for support when you need it, and remain conscious of every decision. In the end, it's all about choice, *choosing* to have the self-discipline to avoid debt in the first place or to climb out of it. The opposite scenario is one where all choice is extinguished, when financial quicksand forces your practice to close and your retirement years wind up meager.

Debt is not a good place to allow poor planning or collegial one-upmanship to lead the way. Keep this philosophy in mind as you navigate the choppy waters of good and bad debt.

# PART II:

# A GUIDE TO WEALTH PRESERVATION

# CHAPTER 3:

# INVESTING FOR YOUR FUTURE

*"**Compound interest** is the eighth **wonder of the world. He who understands it, earns it ... he who doesn't ... pays it.**"*

**- Albert Einstein**

Investing wisely in stocks, bonds, or other securities is a key component to optimizing your long-term financial security. Especially if you invest over a long period of time, you can weather market fluctuations and watch your money grow. The other good news: the rate of return of the capital markets is more than 10% over time.[7] Seems like a no-brainer, right? Well, yes. But designing an optimal investment portfolio requires careful planning, analysis of your goals, and a clear-eyed self-awareness.

While long-term investing in the markets can mean sailing into a comfortable retirement, *how* you invest – how much money you allocate and where, your age, and your tolerance for risk – must be taken into account in order to create a portfolio that best reflects your goals. Many chiropractors tend to be risk averse (not adverse). Busy with managing both patients and the business of running a practice – not to mention all the various products being pushed at them – the idea of diving into something as intangible as the stock market can be intimidating.

With the right team in place to help you form a plan, and a willingness to stick with it, those feelings of intimidation can transform into the satisfaction of financial security for the future.

## YOUR ATTITUDES TOWARD RISK

"Black Tuesday." "The Great Recession." Investors cringe recalling the dozen or so significant market corrections of the past century. While we can do a great deal to mitigate risk, we cannot eliminate it. In any investment plan, it is important to understand both the types and the amount of risk you are taking on and to be sure that you are comfortable with that plan. This understanding will greatly increase your ability to adhere to your long-term investment plan and increase your chances of achieving your financial goals.

Your optimal level of risk depends on both your personal preferences and your situation. Here are the three components of risk assessment:

1. Risk Tolerance: Your Response to Market Fluctuations

Over the course of your investment life, the value of your portfolio will rise and fall. While we would always rather see our portfolio value rise, a prudent investor knows that any investment will have some periods in which the value will fall. Equity markets, in particular, are volatile and investors must expect that there will be regular periods of rising prices and regular periods of falling prices.

Your risk tolerance describes your level of comfort in waiting through the downturns. If the risk you take is within your risk tolerance, then you will be able to maintain your investment strategy through both strong markets and weak ones, giving you the best chance of investment success.

2. Risk Aversion: Your Vulnerability to Losses

Designing an appropriate investment strategy requires understanding and weighing factors that can be in conflict.

Your tolerance for risk may be high, but as a prudent investor, you should consider your ability to withstand financial losses. Because market downturns are unpredictable, you need to assess the real economic harm you might face if your portfolio seriously declined in value. If your portfolio failed to provide the returns you had planned for, would you need to adjust your goals?

### 3. Risk Avoidance: Your Need to Take Risk

Most investors would not choose to take more risk than is necessary. While this is a simple statement, investors often fail to build this concept into their investment planning. Your need to take risk is directly tied to your rate-of-return objective.

If you need your portfolio to grow more quickly over your time horizon, you will want a higher rate of return. An increase in your rate-of-return objective, however, will generally mean taking more risk. If your return objective is higher than your risk tolerance (willingness to take risk) or your risk aversion (your vulnerability to losses), then you must adjust one or more of these parameters. This could mean, for example, retiring from your chiropractic practice later and possibly subjecting yourself to the discomfort of greater risk or increasing your savings.

On the other hand, if your rate-of-return objective can be lowered because your assets can support your goals with less growth, then your need to take risk is reduced and your portfolio should be allocated accordingly.

Dr. Ruth Lytton at Virginia Tech and Dr. John Grable at the University of Georgia, both personal finance professors, developed an Investment Risk Tolerance Quiz that can help you gain a clearer picture of your risk tolerance. Take the quiz and see your results at: njaes.rutgers.edu/money/riskquiz/.

## THE POWER OF DIVERSIFICATION

Such a rational analysis of your risk tolerance may fly in the face of our get-rich-quick culture. From TV shows to anecdotes, we've all heard of the guy who bought low, sold high, and made a fortune. When approached this way, the equity market, like Las Vegas, becomes a place of high stakes wins and dizzying losses. While the thrill of the gamble is worth the risk for some, for the long-term investor, this idea of "beating the market" is at odds with a more intelligent academic approach.

The risk and reward characteristics of all of your portfolio's holdings should be analyzed as one, not separately. While you may have heard from a colleague, your Uncle Joe, or even Jim Cramer, that a certain stock is "hot" or "primed to rally," an efficient allocation of capital to specific asset classes is *far* more important than selecting the individual investments.

Smart diversification of your portfolio can mean investing in a variety of stocks or bonds, both domestic and foreign. And, while we often hear "stocks and bonds" referred to in terms of the equity market, what exactly do these two investment types mean? In brief, stocks are shares of individual companies. Often, a successful company looking to expand will seek funds from the financial markets by splitting the company into shares and selling these shares on the open market. Each share represents ownership – however small – of the company, and the value of the shares will rise and fall with the company's fortunes. Bonds, however, represent debt. An entity looking for funds borrows money from the public market and then pays each individual lender interest on the cash it borrows. Upon maturity, the investor is reimbursed the full amount of the original loan on top of the interest earned as the loan matured.

While stocks tend to be more volatile in the short term, they have historically offered superior long-term returns. Bonds usually pay back the full principle at maturity, so are less risky – though they lack the potent punch of stocks' long-term payoff. Because of this difference, a balance between risky stocks and staider bonds is key, though achieving the right balance for you will depend on your tolerance for risk as well as your goals and time horizon.

Your asset allocation – where your money is invested – can determine over 90% of the performance variation of your investment portfolio. How your investment dollars are allocated far outweighs the potential effects of individual security selection and market timing.

This is good news. While some may make a hobby out of obsessing over daily fluctuations in the market, as a busy chiropractor, you likely don't have the time or mental space to worry about each and every stock or bond pick in your portfolio. Happily, you don't have to.

## GOING ABROAD

One key to diversification when you are planning your asset allocation is deciding how much of your portfolio to place in domestic and foreign investments. Global diversification reduces your risk by putting more and varied stocks into your bucket. Consider this fact: while there are 3,500 stocks in the U.S., there are globally around 10,000.

Still, investors typically lean toward a significant home investment bias when building out their portfolios. Why? A preference for the familiar is one reason. As discussed, investing means accepting a certain amount of risk, so investors seeking the comfort of the familiar may feel more at ease in their home markets. As well, some investors feel they are attaining sufficient global diversification by investing in multinational companies based in the U.S. Finally, there is a perception of foreign investments being riskier due to the vagaries of currency fluctuations.

But over time, financial theory holds that global asset diversification can bolster your portfolio more than if you stay in your home market. Of course, you'll want to balance your domestic and foreign investments according to your unique needs.

## THE TIME IS NOW

Smart chiropractors know they should be long-term investors. This often gives rise to the question "How long is long term?" The answer for many investors is simple – your long-term horizon should be as far into the future as possible. Having a long horizon is a powerful advantage because, as an investor, time is your best friend.

For many chiropractors, the most important long-term goal is to achieve financial freedom in order to be able to do what you want. You may also have intermediate-term goals—funding college educations for you children, buying a vacation home, or contributing to a charitable foundation. You may also have goals that reach far into the future—for example, you may wish to leave legacies to you children, grandchildren and even great-grandchildren.

Regardless of the time horizon of your goals, the simple fact remains that the more time you have, the more likely you are to succeed as an investor. There are two reasons for this. The first is the miracle of compound growth. This is the idea that when you put money aside to earn returns, and then reinvest those returns, you have both your original investment and the returns working for you.

The second reason is the phenomenon of risk reduction over time. Time reduces investment risk, especially in diversified portfolios of stocks. It is natural to worry that if you invest in the stock market today, it may go down tomorrow. But if you have a long investment horizon, tomorrow is just one of the thousands of market days during which you will be investing. Over long periods, many of the ups and downs in the market are cancelled out, leaving the broad market trend.

Even with these powerful reasons to set up an investment portfolio today, many would-be investors still procrastinate. The reasons may vary – lack of funds, intimidation of the process, lack of a trustworthy advisor. If you are putting off until tomorrow what you could do today, let the following dramatic scenario illustrate the cost of waiting to invest:

**Initial savings: $10,000**

**Annual savings: $1,000**

**Years of growth: 25**

**Years delayed: 10**

**Rate of return: 6.00%**

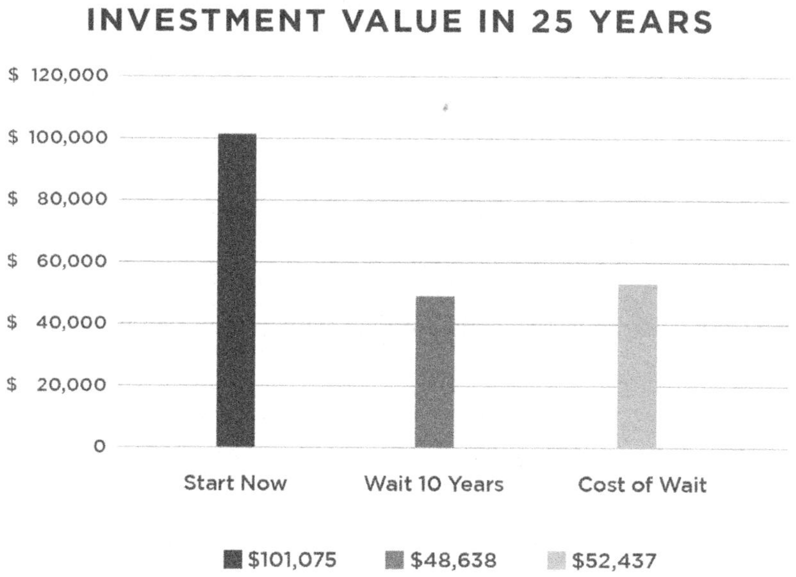


If you start investing now, your initial investment will grow to a value of $101,075 in 25 years. If you wait 10 years before starting this investment, it will grow to $48,683. That's a difference of $52,437! Delay can really cost you.

## GETTING STARTED

Ready to start building your investment portfolio? Great. For most chiropractors, the skill they most excel at is helping people to heal, move more fluidly, or become free of pain. Because these important talents don't necessarily translate into investment expertise, begin by learning the basic terminology and concepts. There are plenty of online resources such as Investopia.com and well-regarded investment books such as *The Only Guide to a Winning Investment Strategy You'll Ever Need* by Larry Swedrow and *Behavioral Investment Counseling* by Nick Murray.

The following five steps will help you design the right portfolio. Congratulations on making today the first day of a more secure financial future! Let's get started:

*The Five Steps of Investing:*

1. Assess your goals and circumstances. The investment plan process begins with honest self-assessment. Examine your financial values and goals, as well as your key relationships, existing assets, other professional advisors, preferred process, and important interests.

2. Set long-term investment objectives. Taking into account the long-term nature of successful investing, set objectives for your portfolio that are appropriate for your willingness, ability and need to take risk, and the investment horizon(s) you identify.

3. Plan your asset allocation. Because it is so important, asset allocation is the first investment decision. During this process, decide how much of your portfolio to invest in each of the

different investment types, or asset classes, including stocks, bonds and short-term investments, both domestic and foreign.

4. Select your investment approach. With an asset allocation in place, select the investment vehicles that you will use to implement your portfolio strategy. Two key investing principles guide these decisions: the importance of diversification and the value of remaining invested.

5. Build your portfolio. Building on the first four steps, construct a portfolio suited to your needs, goals, investment horizons and risk attitude. The building blocks for the portfolio typically are institutional class mutual funds, an excellent way to implement a low cost diversified portfolio.

## WHY MUTUAL FUNDS?

At its most basic, a mutual fund is an investment company that pools the monies of many individuals for the purposes of investing in various securities. Mutual funds are one of the most advantageous investment products for the average investor. Their power: they give small investors access to professionally managed portfolios that are highly diversified. As well, the funds can be redeemed at any time.

Mutual funds have become increasingly popular over the past several decades. In the U.S. in 2016, 9,511 mutual funds managed around $16.34 trillion. Different types of mutual funds contain diverse investment vehicles, which will correspond to the level of risk for each fund. For example, equity funds will primarily invest in common stocks; fixed-income funds will contain mostly bonds and/or money market instruments; hybrid funds will hold some combination of funds.

Mutual funds, while convenient, do cost money. The fund's outlay, which includes transaction fees, investment advisory costs, and marketing and distribution expenses, are passed along to the investors in numerous ways. It's important to understand the fee structure in any mutual fund you choose so that you can avoid any surprises and select the fund that is in alignment with your goals.

There are two broad categories for mutual fund fees: 1) Expense ratios, which are annual fees expressed as a percentage of the fund's average net assets. These monies go to pay for the expenses of running the fund and are typically paid out indirectly by reducing the net returns investors receive. Some funds charge their investors higher expense ratios than others, and these dollars can really accumulate, especially over long periods of time; 2) Loads. These are brokers' commissions that are charged to investors upon purchase or sale of the fund. The time and expertise of the broker in choosing how to invest your money are the justification for loads. A front-end load may mean paying an upfront 5% fee (if you invest $1,000 in a mutual fund, $50 would be taken out as commission, and $950 would then be invested in the fund). Back-end loads are charged when you sell the investment, and typically the amount is tied to the time frame in which you sell. So, if you sold after the first year, a 6% fee would be deducted, but by year seven, the back-end load would disappear altogether.

Other expenses to consider include the tax impact of mutual fund gains, which are taxed yearly on capital gains. Trading costs, too, can whittle away at your returns. Each trade within the fund is associated with a certain cost, so if a manager trades excessively, it can become expensive.

If the various fees associated with mutual funds seem daunting, there are less costly options available. Institutional share class funds are low cost and offer clear advantages to investors. These require a large minimal investment (typically $500,000 or more), so the larger blocks of mutual funds purchased are given a break on many of the above charges. No-load funds are also a more affordable option as these shares are sold directly through the investment company rather than through a second party, such as a broker, thus evading the cost of commissions. In such an instance, the $5,000 you purchase is the same amount invested. Interestingly, research shows that load funds perform no better than no load funds.

The complex and often opaque nature of mutual fund fees can be intimidating, but the convenience of instant diversification that mutual funds provide is a key advantage in any portfolio. Mutual funds are required to publish annual prospectuses outlining the costs, so be sure to look them over to review where your money is going.

# CONCLUSION

Smart and timely investing can set you on course for a bright future because what the returns on your investment really represent is choice – the choice to retire earlier and better, the choice to live debt-free, the choice to pay for your child's college or wedding or grad school.

The power of this is too often offset by fear and busyness and an unfamiliarity of how to get started. But you can stop stalling and take the first step by educating yourself with the numerous and varied resources available. The time is now. As Warren Buffet famously said, "Someone is sitting in the shade today because someone planted a tree long ago." Go ahead and plant your tree today!

# CHAPTER 4:

# CHIROPRACTIC RETIREMENT

*"You are never too old to set another goal or to dream a new dream."*

–C.S. Lewis

Depending on where you are in the lifecycle of your practice, retirement may be a fuzzy, far off vision of ease and travel. Or, it may be beckoning just over the horizon – a call you either welcome or hear with trepidation. Retirement – the when, how, where, and why of easing out of a lifetime's work – is deeply personal, a unique journey for each of us.

For chiropractors, the ability to be in control of when and how you retire is especially crucial. Why? Because this healing profession carries with it some inherent risks that can affect when and how you leave the workforce. A physically demanding occupation, your physical fortitude may in part dictate how long you can practice. As well, most chiropractors are small business owners, so the ability to step away from the daily grind will be directly related to how savvy you have been at managing your practice. The power to retire well requires preparation – years of thoughtful planning that results in the ability to enjoy, even relish, your post-working years.

People are living and working longer than ever before. A recent survey found that 46% of Americans are planning on retiring after age 65, while only 30% expect to retire before it.[8] In a parallel finding, according to the National Board of Chiropractic Examiners 2015 report, chiropractors' longevity in the practice is increasing – 38.3% of practitioners worked more than 25 years in 2014, up from 24.7% in 2009.[9] The good news here is that working longer gives practitioners more time and flexibility to save for retirement.

## PRIORITIZING SAVING

Saving for retirement means different things at different points of your career. It can be tempting to overlook this eventuality when you're young, although the earlier you start saving, the more powerful and flexible your money will be. Chiropractors just out of school are commonly more concerned about setting up or joining an established practice than putting aside money for the far-off future. This is understandable, especially considering the myriad pressures on a young practitioner: school loans and other debts, the outlay necessary to start a practice, and perhaps a young family. But saving early on leverages the power of compound interest to transform even a modest amount of money into a solid nest egg. Consider this: if at age 25 you set aside $286 per month, assuming an 8% return on investment, you will save $1 million by the time you turn 65[10] . In contrast, if you start saving at age 50 at the same rate of return, you would have to set aside $2,413 per month to hit the million dollar mark.

Compound interest means the interest that your investment earns each year is added on to your principle. The result: your balance doesn't just increase – it increases at an exponential rate. To illustrate: if you invest $100 and the interest rate is 8%, at the end of the first year you will have $108. Invest another hundred and now your principle is $208, which at 8% becomes $224.64. Throw another $100 into the pot for your third year and you have $324.64, which at 8% becomes $350.61. Over three years, you've invested $300, and you have received $50 "for free" (the interest). With this simple math, you can see why saving from a young age makes an enormous difference down the road: the longer you play the game, the more your "free" money grows.

Clearly, the power of compound interest is more profound at 25 than at 55. Even so, many professionals still neglect to save money for the future. Amazingly, one in three Americans has saved nothing for retirement – and 56% have saved less than $10,000.[11] Why? More pressing economic concerns and even hardship often play a role, and there's also the enticement to live for the present at the expense of the future. But for ambitious chiropractors especially, it can take discipline to set aside funds that could also be used to expand a business, buy that cutting-edge imaging tool, or take a much-deserved vacation. That said, the initial discipline it takes to start saving right out of school – a rule of thumb is to save 10% of your income – is key because it transforms resistance into habit. And this ability to prioritize saving pays off down the road.

The reality is, setting aside money for retirement doesn't get any easier when you are in your 30's, 40's and 50's as there are always new challenges on the horizon: paying for your children's education, going on vacation with the family, deciding that one spouse stays home to take care of children, or buying a larger house. As you defer saving, the magic of compound interest becomes inverted – now saving 10% of your income is insufficient; 15% or 20% may be necessary to build the funds you need to quit working. As the above example shows, some chiropractors reach their 50s and now must save 30% of their income to have enough money to retire by 65. Unfortunately, in many cases even saving at this higher rate later in life doesn't allow you to enjoy the lifestyle you necessarily dreamed of after your working years. Given how much is at stake, how can we begin to mitigate such a circumstance? According to *Time Magazine*, "Most Americans would rather talk about the birds and the bees than any conversation related to finances."[12] It's time to start talking.

## THE MECHANICS OF SAVING

So, you're committed to setting aside money for retirement. Bravo! This can involve a variety of strategies, depending on your comfort with risk, or vice versa. Keep in mind, investing in any retirement vehicle is a two-step process. First and foremost, you are implementing a tax saving strategy that can save you thousands, and in some cases hundreds of thousands, of dollars in taxes. If that is all you want to do then you can simply stop there and let your money sit in cash inside the retirement vehicle. I don't necessarily recommend this approach, but at a minimum it saves you in taxes.

If you want the money to grow over time, the next step is to decide how you want to invest it. One option is certainly individual stocks or a stock mutual fund, although these are not mandatory inside of a retirement account. Another option is CD's or bonds which perform much differently and have a fixed interest rate and maturity date. Designing a well-balanced investment portfolio of stocks and bonds – and increasing to more bonds as you get older – can be optimal. Investing in the market is commonly thought to garner an 8% return (in reality, it's closer to 5% when adjusted for inflation) over time. Although there is always inherent risk here, diversification between stable and more aggressive choices can mitigate such risk.

Below are several retirement vehicles worth considering.

- **Roth IRA Plan**

  A Roth IRA allows you to set aside after-tax income (up to $5,500 per individual as of 2017), and future withdrawals – including earnings – are tax free. This is an ideal way for new chiropractors to set aside a yearly amount, see compound growth, and then minimize their taxes down the road.

- **Back Door Roth IRA Conversion**

  The Roth IRA has income eligibility limits (for example, in 2017, if you are married filing jointly you can contribute the maximum amount to a Roth IRA only if you make less than $186,000). If you are a high earner, a "back door" IRA conversion is a legal way to get around these limits by converting a Traditional IRA (which has no income eligibility limits) into a Roth IRA.

- **Simple IRA Plan**

  An employer-provided tax-deferred contribution, this vehicle is like a 401(k) but simpler and less expensive. A Simple IRA is a good fit for a small business owner wanting a basic retirement plan for his employees – administrative costs and responsibilities are low. Both employer and employee contribute (maximum contributions are $20,000-$30,000) and owners must be willing to, in addition, fund a small annual mandatory contribution for each employee.

- **SEP IRA Plan**

  This is a type of Traditional IRA that is a simplified way for the self-employed or small business owner to contribute to their own and their employees' retirement funds. In this scenario, employees cannot contribute to the plan. This fund is ideal for owners with no employees seeking to make large contributions (approximately $50,000), or owners willing to contribute on behalf of their employees, perhaps as part of their compensation package.

- **Owner-only 401K**

  This plan can be a good option if your practice does not

employ anyone besides yourself, your spouse or your partner. It is flexible, combining investment options, tax-deductible contributions, and tax-deferred earnings growth. This plan allows each spouse to contribute up to $60,000, saving each of you between $20-25K in taxes depending on your tax bracket. That's $40-50k in tax savings for a couple!

- **Traditional 401k Plan**

  Though the owner must be willing to assume some administrative costs and responsibilities, a Traditional 401K Plan is a good fit for any size chiropractic firm seeking to provide a competitive benefit for its employees. Given the cost and effort, it is important to ensure that the plan will have good participation from the staff. Still, tax savings can be significant as owners can contribute between $50,000 and $60,000, and these assets are protected from creditors.

- **New Comparability 401k Plan**

  This is a custom-designed plan that allows an employer to assign different profit sharing allocations depending on the level (associate, chiropractic assistant, massage therapist, etc.) or criteria (full time, part time) of employees, i.e. the owner may enjoy a 20% rate, while the associate garners 10%. New Comparability plans maximize owner contributions while minimizing the amount the employer needs to contribute to each employee. These work well for companies who have older owners due to the significant tax savings it offers: if you are over 50 years old, in some cases you can contribute up to $60K in pretax money – a tax savings of $20,000 to $25,000 per year, depending on the tax bracket.

- **Defined Benefit Plan or Cash Balance Plan**

  Like a traditional pension plan, these investments are professionally managed. These plans work best for consistently-profitable firms with older owners and younger employees where the employer has a desire for large contributions anywhere between $50,000 and $200,000. Contribution limits increase with age, which allows older, high-earners who perhaps didn't save enough earlier in their careers to set aside generous pre-tax amounts. For example, a married (filing jointly) doctor who earns $600,000 in adjusted gross income ($550,000 wages/$50,000 investment income) will pay $180,500 in federal taxes. BUT with a $200,000 Cash Balance contribution, he'll only pay $103,400 in federal taxes: a tax savings of $77,100 in ONE year!

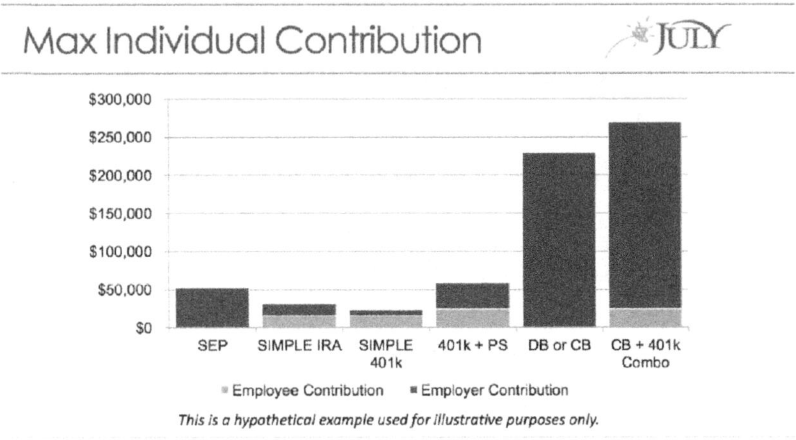


As you can see from the above chart, each of these plans offers a range of outcomes, depending on your age, the size and structure of your business, as well as how much you are able to contribute in order to take advantage of the tax savings each vehicle offers. The choice of retirement product is highly individualized and, given the complexities, it can be wise to consult a trusted adviser to help you assess all the costs and benefits.

A smart, well-timed real estate purchase can also mean a significant payoff down the road (though, clearly, recent history has proven caution and careful calculation are a must when betting on real estate). Purchasing a property that will grow in value can bolster your retirement savings if you understand how to value and purchase real estate. This is often done in a silo by itself and not incorporated into the rest of the financial plan. I am a believer in the power of smart real estate investing and have personally purchased a number of properties that have performed well for me over the years.

Still, investing in real estate poses questions: Was this choice simply made out of fear of investing in the stock market? Was there an actual projected return on this money calculated? Did you overpay for the property because you "needed" to find a place to put your money? Does the plan take into account ongoing, unexpected expenses like vacancies, a new roof, HVAC repairs, driveway, painting, etc.?

Often, I see the non-professional investor not evaluating the inherent risk versus other types of investments like a balanced (stock/bond) portfolio. I hear many chiropractors say they don't want to be invested in the stock market because they lost money in the past so they turn to real estate. Playing the real estate market can seem 'sexy' and appealing because, unlike a stock or bond, you can walk through a condo or imagine how that new coffee shop on the corner will anchor an up-and-coming neighborhood. Online tools like Zillow and Trulia can make the most prudent of us feel like experts spouting the latest comps. And, indeed, a smart purchase can pay off at the end of the day. But, like any investment, preparation and wise counsel are key to a successful outcome.

## WHY THE RUBBER DOESN'T MEET THE ROAD

Clearly, there are many options for saving for a secure and fulfilling retirement – some bolder, some more conservative. Financial advisors and real estate brokers are ready and eager to help. Books are constantly being published touting your ability to retire "happy," "sooner than you think," "smart," and even "wild and outrageous." So where is the disconnect? Why do so many people neglect to save for their futures?

According to *The Strategic Chiropractor*, only 5% of chiropractors can afford to retire by age 65.[13] This dismal statistic points to some hard truths of being a practicing chiropractor: for all the healing done for others, too rarely do chiropractors focus on ensuring their own futures. After all, chiropractors are trained to work with the human body – a much different skill set than running a business or investing wisely. When faced with the practicalities of payroll, hiring and firing, bookkeeping, and insurance, many chiropractors feel overwhelmed and out of their depth. Cash flow struggles are common for chiropractors, especially those who are in the midst of building their practices. Late payments and customer retention are more top of mind than setting aside retirement money. The money is needed *now* – just to keep the lights on.

Here, two scenarios diverge. In the first, many chiropractors grossly underestimate how much they will need to retire. They assume that, given what they've saved in Social Security, along with some modest investments or savings, they'll be fine. But with life expectancy rates of 78.8 years of age for men and 81.2 years of age for women, and assuming you retire around 65, that's a lot of years to support yourself on a fixed income. Also, it's not hard to imagine the longevity of chiropractors extends beyond these averages, given their focus on health and wellness. It's easy to think, "Oh, I've saved $1 million so I have plenty of money to live on for the rest of my life." This may or may not be the case, but you won't know for sure until you've run the numbers and taken into consideration things like health care, inflation, periodic car purchases, vacations and much more. And these concerns are all on top of general living expenses.

Rules of thumb like having 75% of your current income on hand can be misleading because it easily leaves out so many different aspects, especially inflation. Right now our health care inflation assumptions are 6%. Most retirees will pay the medicare premium, drug coverage premium, purchase a supplemental policy, and have some out of pockets costs. This is currently around $12,000 per year for a couple. Assuming health care costs go up 6% per year (which is low, based on recent increases in healthcare costs), this would be over $20,000 per year for a couple in 15 years for healthcare costs alone.

Being unprepared for the realities of your expenses in retirement is scary enough. But worse, for many chiropractors, is a second scenario – they haven't considered retirement saving at all. In a recent survey of 120 chiropractors of varying ages, only 37% listed "Having enough money to live off in retirement" as a concern. Distracted by the daily tasks of running a business, seeing clients, and trying to live well in the present moment, they typically don't prioritize saving until they are getting close to retirement age. By then there are limited options, such as working longer or trying to live on less than they are used to. And this is unfortunate, because even though they now have ample time to engage more with the world through travel and new experiences, there's no money with which to do it.

## CASE STUDY #1: ALL THE RIGHT MOVES

Joel began his professional life working for a chiropractor he admired. When he went out on his own to start a niche practice targeting athletes with sports injuries, he found much success in the health-conscious San Diego area. The practice grew quickly with collections of about $650,000 per year. He retired three years ago at age 65, when his wife Melissa retired from teaching at age 63.

Dr. Joel was forward thinking about the selling of his business and planning for retirement. 15 years prior to retiring, he put his plan in motion, offering his three associates the ability to buy into his practice each year they were with him. He truly valued his staff and showed it in the above-average wage he paid them along with his genuine interest in their well being. After all, Dr. Joel looked at his practice as an enterprise – not something that he was going to sell for pennies on the dollar at the last minute. He understood that if associates weren't nurtured they would, more than likely, leave and start their own practice, and his time and money invested in them would be wasted.

Too often, chiropractors make empty promises to their associates that they will eventually sell the firm to them down the road. But at Dr. Joel's practice, although it was a very small percentage of ownership initially, his colleagues' ability to buy shares gave them the confidence that their time and energy invested there would pay off. Compounding the forethought of this plan, many chiropractic firms suffer when the primary doctor loses his passion for the business that he had in the early years. With the associates having ownership in the practice, they have a vested interest in seeing it continue to grow. After all, they will be 100% owners soon enough.

With around $3 million in assets, Joel and Melissa had done a good job of setting aside money over the years, including reinvesting the money they received from the periodic sale of shares of his practice to his colleagues. With a conservative (80% bonds and 20% stocks) investment portfolio and Social Security income of $46,000 per year, they want to live conservatively. Assuming they live to be 93, what is the probability that they will be able to enjoy their retirement goals? Let's examine the details.

Their expenses include:

- $95,000 in general living expenses (assuming 3% inflation per year so this number will increase to $135,000 by the time they are 80);
- $12,000 for health care (at 6% Inflation this will increase to $23,000);
- $15,000 per year (no inflation) for vacations for them and sometimes the extended family;
- $40,000 each (no inflation) to purchase a new car every 10 years.

Joel and Melissa were prepared and conservative, so they have a 90% probability of reaching their goals, living their golden years how they envisioned them to be. That said, seemingly small adjustments to the plan could quickly set the ship off course. Consider that if they end up living to 95 instead of 93, the probability of success decreases to 80% - yes, with just a two-year difference! And, if they got a bit carried away with their expenses – eating out too often, splurging on that boat

– and spend $112,000 per year instead of $95,000, their probability of success would go down to 58%.

There are two key take-aways from Case #1: First, even with their relatively high net worth at the start of retirement, this couple will need to spend modestly in order for this money to sustain them into their 90s. Second, it is crucial to consider how inflation affects these numbers over time. Of course, there are many unknowns, especially when it comes to health and longevity, but a conservative approach to spending and attention to detail can give this couple a good chance of a happy retirement.

## CASE STUDY #2: A LEAKY SHIP

Tom has enjoyed a stellar reputation in his Cleveland community for over 27 years. At age 65, he is considering selling his successful chiropractic practice and enjoying his retirement. But his plan is tinged with doubt and fear that if he and his wife live the lifestyle to which they have become accustomed, they will run out of money. Let's get into the details.

Tom makes $225,000 per year, while his wife Nancy, a year younger than her husband, was a stay-at-home mom to their now-grown children – something they both prioritized. They have $1.3 million saved in a 401K and various mutual funds. Between them, they will receive $45,000 in Social Security. While this isn't a bad start, the couple upgraded to a bigger, $750,000 house eight years ago and they will be making mortgage payments of $24,000 per year until Tom is 73. Add to this a HELOC line of $130,000 they took out to make various upgrades on the house and purchase a boat and a new car – and we can see how their debt burden dampens their probability of a well-funded retirement. For Tom to retire at age 67, they must reduce their spending to $85,000 per year – a significant decrease from their current rate of well over $100,000 (not including healthcare and the mortgage). Even so, their chances of achieving their retirement goals of living well to 88 (him) and 90 (her) is only 78%. Tom will have to work until he's 70 in order to increase their chance of success to 90%.

But Tom wants to retire soon. The physical demands of the job were making it hard for him to treat clients the way he would like to, and he's feeling ready for the next stage in life. To this end, he spoke with a broker to help him sell his practice. Surely the profits made from the sale of such a reputable, well-appointed business (over 230 patients per week!) would help him pay off his debts and sail with Nancy into the proverbial sunset. The collections from the practice are in the $400,000-$500,00 per year range, so the broker is listing it for $500,000 with the hopes of attracting an eager practitioner looking to take the reins. But here Tom is making a common mistake in assuming his practice will sell for around 1x his annual collections. Indeed, they usually sell for much less.

Tom has long enjoyed a high standard of living due to his comfortable income. This fact makes it even more difficult to swallow the hard financial realities of retirement. Even with decent savings, a significant debt burden and an uncertain real estate prospect can significantly decrease the chances for long-term stability. Tom's story highlights the danger of overspending in the years leading up to retirement. Ideally, retirement planning begins right out of school, but especially in one's 40s and 50s, the future should always be top of mind.

## DANGER! DANGER!

If you assume your chiropractic business is going to leave you with a large lump sum of cash when you sell it at retirement, think again. When selling a practice, too often the expectations do not align with the realities. The fact is, most chiropractors who rely on the sale of their business to fund their retirement are forced to either retire with meager funds or work longer than they had anticipated. Why?

One reason has to do with the realities of the post-Great Recession lending market. A young, ambitious chiropractor, likely saddled with his own school debt, is simply not going to be able to borrow what he needs to purchase a half a million dollar practice. According to Dr. James Fedich, author of *Secrets of a Million Dollar Practice*, a single-doctor practice would be lucky to sell for 80% of its annual gross collections. And that's the best-case scenario, as many go for much less. There is much involved in selling a practice – location, condition of equipment, staff and client retention, negotiating a buy-in or co-ownership, and more. A professional practice broker can appraise your practice in order to assess its true market value so you can approach selling with your eyes wide open.

## HELP IS ON THE WAY!

Like the body, everyone's financial life is unique and requires a steady maintenance regimen. Your money and your priorities change over time, and – to continue the metaphor – need more than a one-time adjustment. As a chiropractor, you understand the danger of self-diagnosis. In financial matters, and especially a crucial concern like a happy and secure retirement, it's no different.

Few chiropractors (regardless of their levels of education and intelligence) should be their own investment managers, let alone "Wealth Manager." Strategizing for your optimal retirement in conjunction with a well thought out and written investment plan is constant and demanding work. And it often can require nerves of steel during difficult market conditions. How many chiropractors, at the end of a hard day of work and with precious little time, will have enough energy, focus, and cool perspective to manage the investments that are key to their financial futures?

For many chiropractors, hiring a trusted wealth manager who can be a true partner in planning for the future is at first intimidating, but then garners feelings of massive relief and fewer sleepless nights. When your money is in the hands of an expert, one who is coordinating with your accountant, lawyer and insurance professional, nothing falls through the cracks. And you can focus on what you are truly passionate about – healing.

# CHAPTER 5:

# PRIORITIZE YOUR FUTURE WITH A SMART EXIT STRATEGY

*"And in the end, it's not the years in your life that count. It's the life in your years."*

**–Abraham Lincoln**

It's inevitable: someday, in some way, you will leave your practice. You may retire, change careers, encounter health difficulties, or decide to work part time. Depending on where you are in your career, this departure may happen far in the future, or be just around the corner. But it will happen. For this reason, making an exit strategy is a key part of your business plan – one that is crucial to you and your family's financial well-being. Yet many chiropractors tend to procrastinate on this issue. Interestingly, fewer than 30% of small business owners create a concrete, workable plan to transition out of their businesses. And a mere 5% of chiropractors can retire by age 65 and maintain their current lifestyle.[14]

The reality is, even the *lack* of a solid exit strategy is still a plan… it's just a bad one. This "no plan" plan may be due to fear, lack of knowledge and resources, or unfounded hope that it will all somehow sort itself out. Whatever the reason, not having an exit plan in place can have serious repercussions down the line. Whether your practice is thriving or just middle-of-the-road successful, now is the time to prioritize your future and create a tangible strategy for leaving your business successfully.

**What an Exit Strategy Really Means: Freedom**

With the "no plan" plan, you will most likely become a casualty to things over which you have little to no control – economic currents, industry trends, and your own health. On the other hand, doing the hard work of creating an exit strategy gives you both control and freedom. Why? Because proactively working towards the best possible transition will most certainly leave you with more financial resources at your disposal than if you just play it by ear and hope for the best.

Most chiropractors possess an entrepreneurial spirit, meaning they value freedom. This love of freedom is perhaps what sparked that initial fire to pursue this healing art. A plan for transitioning out of your practice is the next iteration of this love of autonomy: call it Freedom 2.0. Do you dream of a second career, or travel, or slowing down and simply spending time with your family? Is your hope to buy a second home in a lovely locale or to fund your grandchildren's college education? These choices are a luxury, the direct result of the work you take on *now* to create a smart plan for your future. And, the sooner you plan, the more freedom you will have.

## THE PITFALLS OF THE "NO PLAN" PLAN

There are several reasons chiropractors tend to delay planning their transition into retirement or a second career. First, like other professionals, it can feel depressing to think about exiting the 'prime' years of career-building and beginning a new phase of life where, let's face it, one's eventual death must be considered. Also, selling or passing on a business can feel akin to losing a child – you've spent years nurturing your practice so it follows that leaving it behind can be painful. Finally, you love your work! Why would you want to quit the daily pleasure of helping people? It can be difficult to imagine a time when you may not feel as passionate about your practice as you do today.

Aside from these emotional hurdles, planning a solid exit strategy can be time consuming and intimidating. For a busy chiropractor managing the day-to-day, it's tempting to procrastinate this issue in favor of putting out the daily fires of cash flow glitches and client retention. Many a successful chiropractor has said to himself:

"I love my job and am proud of what I've built. Maybe I'll just never retire!"

Or,

> "I love my job and am proud of what I've built. I'm sure my associate will want to take over the practice someday. I'll talk to her about that at some point."

Or,

> "My practice is really booming! No doubt I can sell it for a bundle when I'm ready to retire."

Do any of these sound familiar? If so, beware. These "no plan" assumptions are based not on reality, but rather on unfounded optimism. If you're a chiropractor who never wants to retire, you may want to consider how you'll feel about adjusting spines when you're 75 and slowing down physically. And assuming an associate will be on board for taking over when the time is right for you, is putting your future in the hands of someone who may not share your vision. Indeed, most practices that are passed on to the next owner without a solid plan in place will fail.

Finally, and most commonly, without foresight, careful planning and patience, counting on the traditional sale route for a practice is dicey at best. Understanding the exact value of your mature practice is difficult to parse – 65 percent of business owners do not know their company worth.[15] And, as discussed in Chapter 4, many chiropractors fail to sell even the most successful practices for the hoped-for windfall they were counting on to retire comfortably. Either they wait too long to sell – when either their health or the business is in decline – or market forces hinder their ability to maximize the value of the business.

As many chiropractors succumb to the assumptions listed above, they miss the window where they can sell at the *right time to the right person for the most profit.* Rather than waiting for your practice to decline, it needs to be performing at its most optimal when you prepare to sell. Other conditions beyond your control can also work in your favor, such as the chiropractic industry performance as a whole. Transitioning at the right time is a moving target, a bullseye that – if you put in the work to hit it – will maximize the money you walk away with.

Resisting the "no plan" plan takes resolve – and help. And that is yet another reason many chiropractors who know they need a concrete exit plan still resist taking the steps to put one in place. They may ask themselves: *Where do I begin? Who do I call? Who can I trust with my most personal financial information?* Just as you assembled your team of advisers when you began your practice, a solid exit strategy may also necessitate professional help as you gather the data necessary to strategize a positive transition.

## THE FIRST STEP: INFORMATION GATHERING

The first task in creating a savvy exit strategy is arming yourself with concrete data that will inform your options. This includes how your practice has been performing for the past three years or so, and what it is currently worth. The hard data you gather will provide an unvarnished look at the market value of your practice, including the amount of money a bank will (or won't) be likely to loan a prospective buyer. An appraiser who specializes in the chiropractic industry will look at your services, equipment, profit and loss statements, as well as market forces in your geographical region, and provide a reasonable estimate of what you can expect from the sale of your business.

The other important piece of this information gathering is admittedly more fun. What do you want to do in your retirement or second act? And, it follows, how much money will you need in order to achieve this dream comfortably? Timing will be a key piece of the puzzle here. After all, someone who wants to get out of chiropractic at 55 to pursue another career will have much different financial needs than a doctor who wants a quiet retirement at 70 or one who wants to retire at 70 and travel the world. Your approximate needs post-transition will inform your options as you move forward. The sweet spot will be transitioning in such a way that it optimizes your chance of achieving these dreams.

Having all of this information in hand is like pulling back the curtain to reveal the reality of your situation. While it can be tempting to rely on assumptions, hope, and anecdotal evidence, hard data is a far more powerful and effective way to plan your future. (If there are investments or retirement funds that have been growing for you, these should be taken into account as well.) Think about it: if the sale of your practice will not earn you enough to retire comfortably, wouldn't you want to know that now, rather than face this unpleasant reality down the road where the options are fewer and less appealing?

# FINDING YOUR EXIT STRATEGY SOUL MATE

Unless you decide to simply liquidate your business (an admittedly quick, though financially dubious option), your successful transition will rely on the person who will be taking over your practice. Who is this all-important individual? Ideally, you'll hand the keys off to a trusted associate who is eager to take your baby to the next level. Or, an enthusiastic up-and-comer buys you out for a tidy sum. (Cue scene of you driving off into the sunset.)

But too often the reality of finding the ideal prospect for your practice is not so simple. (Which is, again, why planning early for your transition is wise: more time equals more options.) For many chiropractors, finding the right person to take on their practice is the most challenging part of a successful exit. The chiropractic industry is facing some intractable challenges that make passing on your business especially challenging. Here's an unfortunate demographic reality: as ever more baby boomers retire (the average DC is 57-59 years old – a baby boomer), there are simply not enough young people coming out of chiropractic school to replace them. Indeed, for every 10 chiropractors looking to get out, there is only one wanting in.[16] This clearly translates into a buyer's market where a younger chiropractor looking to purchase a practice has his or her pick – and plenty of negotiating power.

Some lucky doctors have the opportunity to pass on their practice to a known associate willing to take over and continue building the business. This is an ideal situation, but one in which planning and implementation should begin early, on paper, and with legal support. Communication regarding mutual expectations and timing should be ongoing and above-board.

I emphasize continued communication because simply assuming your associate will gladly step in when the time is right for you can lead to disappointment and unhappy surprises. Without something in writing, your associate has no reason to take the vague promise of future ownership seriously. And, given the market realities discussed above, younger associates enjoy the freedom to switch practices or purchase a perhaps more attractive business when the time is right for them. Here again, assumptions and hope and ambiguous "understandings" are the enemy. Your future depends on agreements on paper and hard, cold data.

Spend time getting to know your likely prospect – her needs, expectations, and financial viability. (Even if this is a long-term associate, actively engage in discussions regarding the potential sale.) Although it can be tempting to thrust a contract under her nose and hope for the best, assessing compatibility before anyone has a formal agreement in hand can help you to avoid late-stage disappointment. If you sense at this point that there is a misalignment, it's best to move on rather than waste time on a deal that's likely to fail.

## NEGOTIATING YOUR TRANSITION

Once you have found a likely prospect, it can feel like freedom is just around the corner. But navigating the actual contractual and financial negotiations goes beyond a simple quid pro quo deal, especially if the sale is complex. Here, many deals do indeed fall apart for several common reasons.

1) ***Financing snafus.*** The money has to come from somewhere, and this usually means a bank loan. But assuming a bank will offer full financing trips up many a would-be happy deal. Overly confident doctors agree on a price, and when the buyer learns the bank is willing to pony up less than was hoped for, the parties often assume this is the end of the road. It doesn't have to be so! Rather than going back to the drawing board and finding another prospect (usually the most challenging part of the process), this is an opportunity to continue negotiations based on what the bank is offering or to look for a loan elsewhere.

2) ***Lack of negotiating skill.*** Selling a business is a skill like any other, but most chiropractors (both the buyer and the seller) usually have little experience in the matter. For this reason, common sales objections are too often met with throwing in the towel. But pushback from the opposing party in a deal this significant is going to happen. It doesn't mean the negotiation has to fall apart; it's all part of the back-and-forth dance of the deal.

3) ***Stalls.*** Allowing a deal to stall out often leads to a failed transition – and is also usually due to inexperience. At every point in the negotiation, there needs to be a smooth path to the next phase. Hurdles should be dealt with in a timely manner, with thoughtful Plan B's at the ready in order to swiftly move the prospect along. Think of a successful sale as a boat that moves quickly along with the river's current. Getting caught on a rock or branch can too easily upend your vessel.

Whether you are selling to an outside prospect or an associate, the day you sign the contract will surely be a happy one. Keep in mind, however, there are often a slew of post-transaction details that may keep you involved in the practice for weeks, months, or even years in the case of the most complex sales. As much as possible, pre-planning the transfer of insurance, payroll issues, and addressing inevitable knowledge gaps in the day-to-day running of the business can lessen this period.

# YOUR SECOND ACT

Welcome to Freedom 2.0! With proper planning, you have now made a successful exit from your practice. You likely won't miss the paperwork, staff headaches and daily pressures of running a business. But that may not mean you are ready to curl up on your easy chair with the remote. Many chiropractors eschew the idea of a traditional retirement that involves slowing down, golf, or some other laid-back pastime.

A second part time or full time career will, of course, depend on your age, financial and health realities, as well as your family responsibilities. But it could involve writing, coaching, real estate, or whatever activity excites you and makes you feel vital. Some chiropractors are keeping a toe in the chiropractic water with the popular "Sell & Switch" concept. Here, you sell the practice to your associate but continue to be involved in the practice as an associate yourself. The advantages to this scenario are obvious: there are less administrative headaches, yet you still enjoy patient interaction and avoid the harsh brake screech of your career.

Hopefully, with the money you have made from the profitable sale of your business, you can pursue whatever second act strikes your passion. This luxury is the happy ending of a successful exit strategy.

*I am indebted to Tom Necela, DC for many of these insights.*

# PART III:

# ENHANCING AND PASSING ON YOUR WEALTH

# CHAPTER 6:

# TAX MITIGATION FOR CHIROPRACTORS

*"An investment in knowledge pays the best interest."*

**- Benjamin Franklin**

Complying with Federal Income Tax regulations is a necessary burden we all must face. For chiropractors, tax liability tends to cause significant anxiety because many are small business owners (one in three chiropractors is self-employed[17]), which puts the responsibility of setting aside money for taxes squarely on their shoulders. This obligation, in addition to the pressure of running a business, caring for patients, and marketing their services to the community, can feel onerous.

Tax anxiety means too many sleepless nights for this healing profession. And tax overpayment can lead to decreased cash flow, less peace of mind, and delayed retirement. How can we better handle this inevitable issue, and face it with smart planning rather than dread? There is a solution: support from a trusted advisor, coupled with self-discipline, can mitigate the stress of taxes, as well as the amount you pay.

## COMMON TAX MISTAKES

In a recent survey of 119 chiropractors, 34% said they were worried about taxes when it comes to their personal financial future. Even so, many chiropractors fall victim to tax missteps that cost them considerably. Setting aside money for taxes takes discipline. Self-employed chiropractors must pay a 15.3% self-employment tax, in addition to income tax, on all or a portion of their income, which covers Social Security and Medicare. Let's face it, there are a lot more satisfying ways to direct your cash flow, and it can be easy to justify purchasing a new piece of equipment or moving into a bigger office space (after all, these things bring in new customers!) rather than setting aside money for taxes. It can also be tempting to see any surplus cash in your business account as a "net" rather than "gross" paycheck. Promising yourself you'll set aside tax money later and using the cash for a more pressing need (or want) is understandable – especially for a growing practice.

But this issue of expense management too often backfires because when annual or quarterly taxes come due, the coffers are empty, and money for the IRS must be borrowed from elsewhere. Thus begins a cycle of debt that can risk the very business you are fighting to make a success.

Another common tax mistake for the busy chiropractor is the assumption that purchasing equipment that qualifies as a business expense will necessarily make a good return on investment. Gadgets are fun. And any doubt regarding the necessity of the new ergonomic chair or ultrasound therapy system can be quieted with a simple, "Don't worry – I'll write it off!" But a closer look at the math reveals that if, say, the $10,000 machine saves you $1,000 in taxes, that's still a $9,000 outlay on something that may or may not be worth the investment. Could there be a better use for that money? Funding your retirement, perhaps?

These mistakes are avoidable, if understandable. After all, adopting a smart tax strategy may be on your long list of things to accomplish, because right now you're attempting a difficult feat – running a successful medical practice. The key, though, is to understand how these two things are mutually dependent.

# DIFFERENT COMPANY STRUCTURES AND THEIR TAX IMPLICATIONS

Let's start at the beginning. At the outset, any small business must choose a legal entity under which to operate – and this can have a significant impact on your tax burden. And beyond how much you will pay the IRS, the choice of entity will affect how much paperwork you're required to file, your personal liability, as well as your practice's ability to raise money. Given the complexities and tax implications now and down the line, it can be wise to consult an adviser before choosing how to structure your practice. Below is a summation of the pros and cons of each business structure.

**Sole Proprietorship**: This is the simplest business structure, especially if you are one individual going it alone. In this scenario, you are not required to set up a separate legal entity; income and expense are simply included on your personal income tax return. However, choosing to be a sole proprietor has one significant drawback: as the owner, you are exposed to unlimited personal liability for any business risk. For most medical professionals, this lack of legal recourse usually makes being a sole proprietor a non-starter.

**Single Member LLC**: This structure is becoming more popular, as it combines the limited liability of a corporation with the tax ease of the solo practice. With the limited liability company, income and losses pass through to the sole member, who also enjoys liability protection. A single member LLC is one step up from a sole proprietorship, offering the same affordability with an additional level of liability protection.

**Partnership**: Partnerships – where the practice is owned by two or more people – can take several forms. It may be a general partnership where each doctor manages and assumes the obligations of the practice. Or, a limited partnership may have one general partner who runs the show, while the other partners have a limited investment – and liability burden. The tax advantage here is that the partnership itself pays no income tax; income from the practice "passes through" to the individual partners. The downside, however, is twofold – partnerships are more expensive to establish and maintain, and, like the sole proprietorship, general partners are personally liable for any business risk.

**S Corporation**: An S Corporation is a more complex entity wherein stock is issued to each of the owners (not to exceed 100 shareholders), who are then protected from many types of business liability. Profits and losses from the practice pass through to the shareholders, making it appealing, tax-wise, as there is only one level of income tax to pay (unlike C Corporations which incur double taxation). The downside is that S Corporations are subject to an array of rules and regulations, including filing articles of incorporation, holding shareholder meetings, keeping corporate minutes, and following IRS rules regarding reasonable compensation. (Reasonable compensation means the owner/s must compensate themselves appropriately, rather than pass a disproportionate amount of funds through the business with the aim of avoiding Social Security and Medicare taxes.) Professional counsel is a must should you pursue this type of structure.

**Personal Service Corporations**: This structure allows professionals such as chiropractors, professional athletes, and entertainers, to incorporate because of their liability concerns. The IRS labels these entities PSCs and uses a punishing 35% flat tax rate to deter people from using a corporate entity to shelter part of their income. For this reason, PSCs are rarely used today. Should you have a legacy PSC, consult your adviser to switch your practice over to an S-Corp. It will put you in a lower tax bracket every time.

Here's a timeless truth: things change, so it is important that your team of advisers keep you updated on any changes that may impact your entity structure. Your business may be earning much more than it did five years ago; perhaps you've taken on a partner or two; it could be that the tax law has changed. Keeping a watchful eye on whether your legal entity still works for you will help you attain and *maintain* the most advantageous tax strategy.

## CASE STUDY: BOOMING PRACTICE, SLEEPLESS NIGHTS

From an outside perspective, 46-year-old Roger is living the dream of a successful chiropractor. His booming practice collects around $600,000 per year; his family lives in a lovely townhouse in Richmond, Virginia, and he owns a beach house a few hours' drive away. Roger leaves his tax preparation to his CPA, and concerns himself with the day-to-day of his business. But, late at night, there's something that nags at him. He suspects that he's overpaying in taxes and that it's hurting his long-term financial goals.

Roger is right. He could be smarter about his tax obligations, but the way his practice is currently structured means he's paying the IRS more than necessary. Let's break it down. Roger is set up as a sole proprietor, which means he's paying ordinary income taxes as well as FICA on $127,500 of his $300,000 take home pay – 15.3%, or $19,507 per year. (As essentially the employer and employee, he is responsible for Social

Security and Medicare (FICA). The remainder of his income ($172,500) is taxed at a rate of at least 2.9%, totaling $5,003. His total annual tax burden is therefore $24,510.

If Roger instead switched his legal entity to an S-Corp, he would be able to pay himself a reasonable salary (from which he would owe FICA and FUTA) and then take profit distributions from the remainder as a shareholder, on which he would only be required to pay ordinary income tax. If, say, he paid himself a salary of $100,000, he would owe $15,300 in self-employment taxes. However, for the remaining $200,000 taken as a pass through distribution, while this amount would still be subject to income tax, he would not be required to pay self-employment tax on it. In essence, setting up his business as an S-Corp would save Roger over $9,200 in taxes each year.

As mentioned above, tax mitigation and running a smart business are intertwined. These savings, with proper planning, could go towards addressing some of Roger's other concerns for his practice. For instance, he has a 401K plan set up for his three employees, but doesn't make contributions for himself. This tax savings could go towards funding his 401K plan, allowing him to retire sooner and with more money to live the life he desires. As well, feeling it was a bit pricey, Roger currently has no disability insurance, leaving him vulnerable should he suffer an injury or chronic ailment. His tax savings could also help cover disability premiums. Finally, another smart move would be paying down the two mortgages Roger carries – ideally before he turns 65.

Roger's case exemplifies two things: 1) the importance of choosing the right legal entity for your current needs, and 2) tying together the complexities of tax mitigation with your larger overall business goals. This latter issue especially highlights how crucial it is to seek out the right advisor to help guide you. Many CPAs, like Roger's, handle paperwork with little or no thought to the larger implications for their clients' broader life – and future. And, caught up in the details of running a practice, few chiropractors have the expertise or desire to dig into these details. Like Roger, most know they could be paying less in taxes, but are intimidated by the process. A smart financial planner can help.

## TAX MITIGATION BEST PRACTICES

There can be so much fear when it comes to income taxes – fear of authority, paperwork, math, making a mistake, being audited. So how do we get it right? How can we instead approach taxes from a place of empowerment? The answer: knowledge and discipline.

Don't get me wrong: you don't need to become a CPA to make effective decisions about your tax strategy, but a minimum amount of knowledge can go a long way. Questions to inform yourself include: What's your effective tax rate? Will this rate change in the coming year due to a variance in the law or your income? What are your allowable business deductions? Is there a software platform you can use, such as QuickBooks, that can help you stay organized? A shallow dive into your tax situation can be a good first step to feeling in control of your finances. A deeper dive will require the help of a trusted advisor.

So, beyond asking smart questions, what are some best practices for handling your income tax? A good rule of thumb for any business owner: for every dollar you take out of the business – whether it's for groceries, a new car, or a trip – set aside another dollar in a *separate* account for taxes. A big part of being and staying disciplined is simply becoming a creature of habit. If setting aside dollar-for-dollar tax money just becomes something you always do, this financial transaction becomes simply that – a transaction, not a decision. By taking the choice out of the matter, you will be less tempted to justify putting that money towards a want or a need that you feel is more pressing. This account you have *just for taxes* will not only provide you with peace of mind, it will also prevent the regrettable situation of not having enough cash on hand at tax time, and then having to borrow to pay the IRS.

And, here's a bonus: if there is leftover money in the tax account, you can use it to fund your retirement. It's a win-win. Which brings us to another powerful tax mitigation strategy: contributing to your retirement savings. Many people assume a smart way to achieve substantial tax deductions is through business expenses or charitable giving. But these tactics do not ultimately increase net wealth – even if you receive a deduction, there's still an outlay of cash. Consider a $100 charitable contribution that will at best yield a $50 tax deduction. You're still $50 out of pocket. (Please note, I say this not to dissuade you from giving to your favorite cause, but simply as an illustration of financial realities.) If, on the other hand, you use that $100 to fund your retirement account, that contribution is tax deductible. You're not decreasing your net wealth; you're simply moving $100 from one pocket to another – tax deferred or tax free! Simply put, funding your retirement is the most advantageous way you can lower your tax bill.

For some, another smart tax mitigation strategy is enrolling in a health savings account (HSA). Especially given our escalating health care costs and general uncertainty around the insurance market, HSAs can be advantageous because they are owned by the individual. Money contributed to HSAs is not subject to income tax and, if funds aren't used, rolls over from year to year. In retirement, if these funds are not used for medical expenses, they can be withdrawn for any reason without penalty. The one disadvantage here is that HSAs require a high deductible and co-insurance, so are a better choice for those who do not have significant medical expenses.

A tried and true way many small business owners chip away at their tax bill is by deducting their business expenses. This is always a smart strategy, but be careful not to go overboard. You'll need to be able to justify these expenses as necessary for your business needs, which makes sense when we're talking about paper for the copy machine, lunch with a patient referral source, or fees for professional organizations. Less convincing is writing off your spouse's leased car or family vacation to the beach. When it comes to business deductions, common sense goes a long way. And, though audits are rare, keeping meticulous records can help you prove yourself should the IRS come sniffing around. Without paperwork supporting your claims, you may be subject to additional taxes, interest, and penalties.

Many medical professionals who own their practices consider an additional creative strategy for lowering their tax bill: hiring family members in order to shift income to a spouse or a child. Often, it can cost less to employ a family member, especially since a chiropractor doesn't have to pay FICA or FUTA taxes on a child younger than 18. For example, if you hire your 16-year-old to help with the filing and pay her $5,500 per year, this can be a great way to divert your income and begin funding her IRA. A word of warning, however - in order to justify a child's employment, she must actually do the work for which she is hired. An hour here, an hour there chatting with the receptionist after school will not be enough. Be sure to keep a time sheet and note her duties and efforts.

Small business owners may also choose to bring a spouse into the practice, either as an employee or partner. This can lead to tax advantages such as maxing out a 401K plan as the upper limits for annual contributions are now doubled. For example, if you paid your spouse $24,000 she could potentially put 100% of that in a pre-tax employer retirement plan and not pay any ordinary income tax, assuming a 33% tax bracket. (Do keep in mind, however, a primary owner is responsible for payroll taxes even on a spouse's salary. For this reason, seeking tax savings in this manner only truly makes sense when the primary owner is already maxing out what he can contribute to the fund.) Taxes saved through hiring a spouse can perhaps then be used for a well-deserved vacation or to further fund the retirement account.

The key to hiring family members is to remain above board and treat the position as you would if a non-relative were being hired. Not doing so can lead to tax headaches and penalties down the road. According to Craig Aronoff, PhD, co-founder and principal of the Family Business Consulting Group in Marietta, Ga., "Free labor is sometimes worth exactly what you pay for it" if it undermines the practice's finances.[18]

# THE TAX IMPLICATIONS OF REAL ESTATE AND CAPITAL GAINS

Many chiropractors, especially before 2008, either bought their office space or purchased real estate as an investment. As we've discussed, the most advantageous tax move when you have extra cash on hand is to fund your tax-deferred or tax free retirement account. (From one pocket into the other!) But real estate sings a siren song to many professionals – we've all heard the story of the guy who bought the building for $100,000 and sold it for $280,000 five years later.

Simply put – the numbers have to work. Even if you can afford to purchase your office building rather than lease it, this may not be the best way to maximize wealth. For example, if you are paying $5,000 a month in mortgage payments, but you could rent the same place for $2,000 a month, it may make more sense to invest that $3,000 in a retirement fund or even a taxable investment account that is made of stocks and bonds. Yes, you say, but if I own the building I can sell it and retire with a suitcase full of cash! As we've discussed in Chapter 4, that suitcase of cash is more often than not a mirage. Upkeep, a tougher loan environment for buyers, depreciation recapture, and capital gains all work against you.

Capital gains, especially, is a concern when thinking about the tax implications of owning real estate. A capital gain occurs when you sell something for more than you bought it for, and it is subject to federal income tax. When selling business assets, which have been depreciated, a portion of the gain on the sale is treated as ordinary, and thus taxed at a higher rate, rather than capital gains. While you received the benefit of ordinary tax deductions while owning the property, this depreciation recapture is an unwelcome surprise when selling and should be factored into any profitability analysis.

To illustrate, here's an example. Say you decide to purchase your building for $100,000 and five years later sell it for $115,000. While you may do the simple math in your head, expecting to be taxed on $15,000 at the preferred capital gains rate, depreciation can change the formula twofold. First, if for example you took $11,000 in depreciation prior to selling, the actual gain is calculated by subtracting the depreciation from the original purchase price. In this case, the resulting gain would be $26,000 ($115,000 – $89,000). Second, of the $26,000 actual gain, $11,000, or the gain due to depreciation, is taxed at a higher rate. The balance, or $15,000 would be taxed as a capital gain.

Again, when considering a real estate purchase, the numbers have to work. Understanding tax realities is key to making your venture a profitable one – and avoiding unpleasant surprises.

# FINAL THOUGHTS

Many small business owners wonder how much they should fear an IRS audit. The reality is, audits don't happen often (though you should still keep good records and operate within the law). What should be of concern instead is how to strategize, with help from a smart, proactive tax professional, how to avoid overpaying the IRS and ultimately increase your net wealth. With some planning and effort, you may be able to save thousands of dollars. And that money can be diverted to the things that add meaning to your life – investing in your business, your retirement, or pursuing a personal passion.

# CHAPTER 7:

# ESTATE PLANNING 101

*"It takes as much energy to wish as it does to plan."*

– Eleanor Roosevelt

While estate planning may bring up intimidating thoughts of wills and trusts and lawyers, it's actually about one fundamental thing: love. Engaging in the necessary steps to safeguard your legacy for your family doesn't have to be daunting, but many chiropractors tend to procrastinate this issue. After all, you're busy dealing with the stuff of life! Who wants to think about what will happen when you're gone? But if you have a family, a sense of urgency necessarily arises. How can you ensure that your kids or spouse will be ok if you die? Who will provide for them financially? Who will care for them?

With the right guidance and understanding of a few key concepts, you can rest easy knowing you have not only protected your hard-won assets for your family, but also planned for their care and well-being.

## THE BENEFITS OF ESTATE PLANNING

Estate planning is the process whereby you plan and legally prepare for how your assets will be distributed upon your incapacitation or death. While none of us enjoys contemplating end of life issues, the act of estate planning can give you a gratifying sense of control. After all, you've spent years building your practice and accumulated wealth. How these assets are distributed is an important reflection of your life, which is why the word "legacy" is so often used in this regard. What you pass down is not just money – it's a symbol of your devotion and hard work.

Let's break down the benefits of estate planning by examining a worst-case scenario: not planning at all. If you die with no will in place (unfortunately, a situation in which most Americans find themselves) the courts will step in to distribute your assets according to your state's laws. This can be costly both financially and emotionally for your loved ones. Not to mention, there is no guarantee that your wishes (since they were never legally expressed) will be honored. This can be especially detrimental if you have children who are minors. Even if you've had verbal agreements with a favorite sibling or family friend, without your wishes expressed legally, how will these individuals prove to the court that you desired their guardianship for your kids?

Should you become incapacitated, a similar loss of control will occur because the courts must step in to decide who takes care of you, where, and for how long. Given our increasing longevity, it's more important than ever to provide instructions for how your assets should be used for possible long-term care. Without such guidance, a desire to remain at home, or be kept on or taken off a ventilator at a certain juncture, will be unknown or unenforceable.

These grim realities add up to a heavy cost to bear for your loved ones. Which leads me to the primary benefit of establishing an estate plan: it eases the burden for your family. Because your wishes are clear, there are no time-consuming and expensive court visits. Nor are they left with the emotional weight of wondering what you would have wanted, or worse, painful and damaging conflict if family members disagree about who gets what.

Besides making it easier for your family, there are other important benefits of estate planning. These include:

- Tax savings;
- Ensuring dependent family members are taken care of financially;
- Protecting the future of your business;
- Funding a child's education;
- Leaving a charitable legacy.

## PAPERWORK

There are several legal documents involved in estate planning, all of which serve a different function. The Last Will and Testament is the document central to the estate planning process. In it, you will outline how your assets should be distributed upon your death and who will be the executor of these wishes. Assets include personal property, as well as bank accounts or investment accounts. A Will also identifies the desired guardians for your children, should they be minors.

A living trust is another key document. This document allows you to set aside assets in a trust during your lifetime. Until your death, you have complete control over the trust; after your death, the trust is distributed to the beneficiaries according to your wishes. The property within a living trust passes to the beneficiaries without having to go through the sometimes costly probate process (discussed below), which is a key advantage. Another positive aspect is the minimal cost of setting up and maintaining a living trust. It likely costs less than the expense of even one probate proceeding, and only necessitates alteration upon a major life change, such as a divorce or death of the beneficiary.

Finally, a health care directive outlines your desired care, asset allocation for such care, and end of life instructions. It will also appoint the individual(s) you trust to carry out your wishes concerning medical care, pain medication, organ donation, and other final arrangements.

## WHAT IS PROBATE?

Probate simply means the legal process through which assets are passed from the decedent to his or her beneficiaries. Unless you have a large and complex estate, probate tends to be relatively straightforward. A legal notice is created for any outstanding claims from creditors, any unpaid taxes and fees are paid, and the remaining assets are distributed according to your Will. In the event of no will, state law will dictate the distribution of assets. In some cases, probate may include locating beneficiaries or resolving disputes among the heirs. The filing of final state and federal income tax returns for yourself and your estate concludes the process.

Probate is only required for assets listed under your sole name, so it is possible to craft an estate plan that avoids probate and its associated fees entirely. As mentioned above, a living trust is probably the most popular non-probate asset. As well, assets such as life insurance policies and retirement accounts that name a specific beneficiary pass outside of probate. Transfer on Death accounts also avoids probate, as it allows the owner to name a beneficiary(s) for the account upon his or her death. Because assets that fall under probate are in your *sole* name, property or bank accounts with a joint title are also exempt.

## TAX ISSUES

Basically, taxable income earned within the year that you die – whether from your personal earnings, investments, or a trust – will need to be reported to the IRS, and both federal, state, and estate taxes may be due. Tax deferred vehicles such as IRAs and 401Ks are also taxable in the federal estate tax return. However, unless you are a very high earner this is not likely to matter (see below). More important, the beneficiaries of these accounts will have to claim the money they pull out as taxable income. In order to avoid this scenario, one good strategy is to roll these funds into an inherited IRA, which may decrease the tax load for your beneficiaries but depends on a variety of factors, including their relation to you, their respective ages, and when they take out funds. Passing on a non-Roth IRA can be tricky, especially if there is a significant amount of money in the fund. A misstep could be costly for your beneficiary. An experienced financial adviser can help.

The media gives much attention to the Estate Tax, or so-called "Death Tax", which is an additional tax on your assets before they can be passed on to your beneficiaries. As of 2018, this tax only applies to estates worth over $11,200,000, so the majority of people will not feel its effects.

Federal and state tax laws are subject to change, so it's important to consult a knowledgeable estate planning attorney to help guide you through this process.

## WHAT HAPPENS TO YOUR PRACTICE?

An estate plan should take into account that which you've worked so hard to build: your chiropractic practice. After all, it may be the most valuable asset you own, which is why its fate must be considered in your estate plan. If you are a solo practitioner and assume your family will sell the business upon your death, it can be helpful to have a written list of possible candidates who may be interested. But, as I've mentioned throughout the book, chiropractors often overestimate the windfall, or lack thereof, that the sale of their practice will provide. For this reason, a robust, low cost life insurance plan that will provide for your spouse and dependents – no matter what happens with your practice – is crucial.

In the event that you work with a partner or associate, and one of these individuals has the desire and capacity to take over the business if you die or face health issues that prevent you from working, it's smart to create a *written* succession plan. (For more information on exit strategies, see Chapter 5. Another option could be agreeing with a fellow, trusted chiropractor to take over each other's practice should one of you die. Again, any agreement should be in writing.

## CHARITABLE GIVING

Designating that some or all of your assets go to a charitable organization that has personal meaning for you has benefits that go beyond tax deductions. Whether it's funding for a specific scholarship, medical research, public radio, or some other worthy cause, these gifts continue your legacy in a meaningful way after you pass. As well, if you have children, contributing to societal or community good in this way instills in them an appreciation for giving.

While small donations involve simply writing a check, there are several vehicles for passing a more significant portion of your estate on to a charitable cause. You may gift shares of stock or set up a charitable trust where the organization can receive a percentage of the trust while you are alive and get the remainder of the trust upon your death. Another way to give is through a donor advised fund. Simpler and cheaper to set up than a private foundation, in a donor advised fund, a donor can contribute over time and be involved in how the giving evolves. Donor advised funds are not tied to any specific charity, but can change to reflect specific interests, organizations and projects. Besides the tax deductions tied to this giving, these funds require an active role which your children can maintain after your death. This is a lesson in giving that can span generations.

# WHAT WILL AN ESTATE ATTORNEY DO FOR YOU?

Your situation is unique. So it's crucial you find an estate attorney knowledgeable in your state's laws who will sit down with you and carefully listen to your needs. As this person will be privy to your most personal information, you may want to meet with several lawyers before landing on the one with whom you are most comfortable. At the initial meeting, he or she will likely ask you key questions regarding how you want to distribute your assets among family members and at what age/s, guardianship issues, as well as healthcare wishes for yourself.

Even as these questions can be difficult to confront, the risk you face by avoiding estate planning is decidedly worse – for both your bank account and your family's future. Don't wait!

# CHAPTER 8:

# PROTECTING YOUR WEALTH

***"A big part of financial freedom is having your heart and mind free from worry about the what-ifs of life."***

**– Suze Orman**

No one expects to get hurt, sued, flooded, or robbed on the job. These events are outliers, unlikely catastrophes that surely won't happen to you! Maybe not; perhaps you will sail through your career without encountering unexpected loss. But if you do happen to confront calamity, it's important to have the right insurance in place to protect your business and other assets.

Obtaining the proper amount of insurance coverage is important in any industry, and, as a chiropractor, there are several unique considerations to keep in mind. As health care professionals and, often, business owners, liability considerations are paramount. After all, you have your practice, your employees, and your family to protect. Here are the types of insurance it is wise to consider, followed by more detailed descriptions below:

- Disability Insurance
- Life Insurance
- Malpractice Insurance
- Business Owner's Protection
- Auto and Home Insurance
- Umbrella Policies

## DISABILITY INSURANCE

Consider this: at least one in four workers will face some sort of disability during their working years.[19] Few professionals understand this issue like a chiropractor. After all, you treat people suffering from disabling conditions or injuries each day! But what if you yourself becomes disabled? Your job is physical, and either an injury or simply the wear and tear on your body – especially after years of practice – may prevent you from working.

For these reasons, disability insurance is a must for chiropractors. Depending on the plan you choose, this coverage will replace some or all of your income if a disability prevents you from working. You may select either a short-term or long-term disability policy. The former usually covers disabilities for up to six months, while the latter can provide a portion or all of your salary for your lifetime. The cost considerations here are dependent on a variety of factors, including your age, health, lifestyle habits, and amount of benefits you'd like to receive, so it's important to shop around. (The NCMIC offers a plan tailor-made for chiropractors. You can find details at www.ncmic.com.)

## LIFE INSURANCE

If you have a family, you'll need life insurance so your dependents are protected should you die prematurely. Put simply, you'll choose a 10, 20, or 30 year term and if you die within that period, your spouse and children will receive the payout. When choosing a term policy, calculate the amount you will need to replace your income, pay off your debt, and supplement large expenses your family will need to pay in the future, such as college education costs.

Ideally, you'll live a long and healthy life and your family's need for this insurance will end close to when the term expires. By this point, you've been saving and investing and your kids are likely on their own. Your need for life insurance might be behind you.

Beware of gimmicks when it comes to life insurance! Simple term insurance is all you're likely to need. However, many chiropractors are sold expensive whole or variable life insurance policies under the guise of "being your own bank" since you can borrow against their cash value. Agents may expound upon the flexibility of such policies, but don't be fooled. The high premiums on a whole life or variable life policy can be reduced or skipped, but doing so often puts the long-term sustainability of the policy in jeopardy. This leaves many chiropractors having paid in thousands of dollars only to be left with a policy that ends up lapsing.

Beyond a doubt, the better choice is to get simple term life insurance and invest money you would have applied to a more expensive policy into a 401K or IRA. To give you a sense of the price difference, a 40-year-old female could purchase a 20-year, $1 million term policy for around $500-$750 per year.[20] Compare this to a whole life insurance policy that would cost around $10,000 - $12,000 per year. The difference in premiums is the amount she is free to invest in her future. And, depending on the type of retirement vehicle she sets up, she can borrow up to 50% of the account value (maximum of $50,000) with the additional benefit of the interest being paid back to *her* account instead of into the fat pockets of the insurance company.

If you're reading this and have already been duped into a whole or permanent policy, don't worry! There is a smart way forward. If you're approaching retirement, one option is to simply convert the money you've amassed into a less costly hybrid life insurance/long-term care policy. (Keep in mind, a one-time premium payment for a meaningful long-term-care benefit can cost between $50,000 and $75,000.) In the event that you don't need the money for long term care, your family will receive it as part of the death benefit when you die. As with any insurance conversion or termination, be sure that you or your financial adviser understands any potential tax consequences. Additionally, read and understand the fine print, as some policies come with riders attached that limit the exact benefits of long term care.

## MALPRACTICE INSURANCE

Malpractice insurance is a must for any medical practitioner. It covers the costs of a patient's losses or injuries, as well as the associated outlay for any necessary legal defense. Crucially, a robust defense against malpractice suits can safeguard your reputation as a trustworthy chiropractor.

There are two primary instances of chiropractic malpractice: 1) failure to diagnose conditions that require immediate medical attention; 2) damage due to manipulation of body parts that are vulnerable due to previous illness or injury. This last category includes the rare occurrence of patients who suffer a stroke following a cervical manipulation. Though controversial, much objective research has proven this risk is no greater for patients visiting a chiropractor than a general practitioner.

The media tends to bring a bullhorn to the rare occurrence of chiropractic negligence. This sensationalism harms the industry's reputation as a safe and effective means to prevent and recover from pain or injury. In fact, and as a testament to the lack of legitimate suits brought against those in the industry, malpractice insurance rates for chiropractors are among the lowest of the licensed health professions.

## BUSINESS OWNER'S PROTECTION

Especially for the chiropractor who owns his or her own practice, Business Owner's Protection (BOP) is smart to consider. It provides broad coverage of your practice – including the building if you own it, as well as your property within it. Imagine a flood or a fire. With BOP, you'll be confident that you can weather such a misfortune with enough resources to rebuild.

Business insurance includes both property and general liability insurance. It will ideally provide enough protection to: 1) rebuild your property and replace your equipment if there is a loss; 2) shield your assets if you are sued for libel, or someone slips and falls on your property; and 3) keep your business open and running during a misfortune. This latter coverage is key should the daily running of your practice be interrupted. It can provide you with the income you would have made, as well as the cost associated with practicing at a temporary location.

Another advantage to business insurance is that it protects computer records, data files, specialized software and medical equipment. As ever more aspects of running a practice go online or are computer-dependent, their loss can be financially burdensome, especially for a small practice. BOP gives you peace of mind as you grow your business. Should disaster strike, you have sufficient protection to rebuild.

## AUTO AND HOMEOWNERS INSURANCE

Owning a home or a car means you are required to have insurance. Typically, these policies are straight-forward, but in the excitement of purchasing your new house or car it's easy to go with whatever policy details the agent recommends. But do take another look at your deductible. If it's too low (increasing your monthly premium) you're not likely to make a claim because your premiums are sure to rise if you do.

A better plan is to increase your deductible to, say, $1,000 versus $250, pay the lower premium, and still have protection should disaster strike. (And, even smarter: use the money saved on your premium payments to fund an umbrella policy – double protection!)

## UMBRELLA POLICIES

An umbrella policy offers a nice overall back-up that can extend the limits of your other insurance policies. Often more affordable than business insurance, umbrella policies will protect you if you are responsible for a variety of circumstances such as bodily injury, property damage, or if you are being sued for slander or libel.

To dig in a bit, imagine you are involved in a car accident and are responsible for $400,000 worth of injuries to the other driver, but your auto insurance only covers up to $300,000. Your umbrella insurance would cover the remaining $100,000. A smart way to approach this type of protection is to have the coverage match your net worth. So, if you are worth $1 million, buy $1 million worth of coverage. Though this may sound expensive, the premiums are generally very reasonable, given the protection these policies provide.

***

Insurance is, of course, about protecting yourself, your livelihood, and your family. And it is also about peace of mind. With the right amount of coverage in place, you can set any worries aside about possible debacles and focus on what you do best – treating and healing the patients that rely on you.

# ENDNOTES


1 https://www.fundera.com/blog/small-business-statistics

2 Chen, Tim. "American Household Credit Card Debt Statistics: 2014" http://www.nerdwallet.com/blog/credit-card-data/average-credit-card-debt-household/

3 https://www.chiroeco.com/chiropractic-debt/

4 Necela, Tom. The Ultimate Chiropractic Exit Strategy. The Strategic Chiropractor, LLC, San Antonio, TX, 2017.

5 https://www.chiroeco.com/chiropractic-debt/

6 Necela, Tom. The Ultimate Chiropractic Exit Strategy. The Strategic Chiropractor, LLC, San Antonio, TX, 2017.

7 Past performance is not an indicator of future results.

8 http://money.usnews.com/money/blogs/planning-to-retire/articles/2016-06-10/the-most-popular-ages-to-retire

9 National Board of Chiropractic Examiners Practice Analysis of Chiropractic 2015, January 2015.

10 https://www.gobankingrates.com/retirement/takes-save-million-retirement/

11 http://www.foxbusiness.com/markets/2017/01/01/12-jaw-dropping-stats-about-retirement.html

12 http://time.com/money/3892333/couples-money-conversation/

13 https://www.strategicdc.com/products/manual-cd-sets/chiropractic-exit-strategy/

14 Necela, Tom. The Ultimate Chiropractic Exit Strategy. The Strategic Chiropractor, LLC, San Antonio, TX, 2017.

15 Stamey, Josh and Ponder, Greg. "7 common mistakes to avoid when selling a business." The Business Journal. 9/1/17

16 Necela, Tom. The Ultimate Chiropractic Exit Strategy. The Strategic Chiropractor, LLC, San Antonio, TX, 2017.

17 https://bench.co/healthcare/accounting-101-for-chiropractors/

18 http://www.amednews.com/article/20110221/business/302219969/5/

19 http://injury.findlaw.com/accident-injury-law/what-is-disability-insurance.html

20 https://www.nerdwallet.com/blog/insurance/what-is-the-difference-between-term-whole-life-insurance/

Made in the USA
Monee, IL
04 November 2026

67380503R00075